T0327145

"As a pastor, I get asked lots of questions. I'm approached by unbelievers seeking to understand the gospel, new believers unsure about next steps, and maturing believers wanting help answering questions from their Christian family, friends, neighbors, or coworkers. It's in these moments that I wish I had a book to give them that was brief, answered their questions, and pointed them in the right direction for further study. Church Questions is a series that provides just that. Each booklet tackles one question in a biblical, brief, and practical manner. The series may be called Church Questions, but it could be called 'Church Answers.' I intend to pick these up by the dozens and give them away regularly. You should too."

Juan R. Sanchez, Senior Pastor, High Pointe Baptist Church, Austin, Texas

"Where can we Christians find reliable answers to our common questions about life together at church—without having to plow through long, expensive books? The Church Questions booklets meet our need with answers that are biblical, thoughtful, and practical. For pastors, this series will prove a trustworthy resource for guiding church members toward deeper wisdom and stronger unity."

Ray Ortlund, President, Renewal Ministries

How Do I Get Started in Evangelism?

Church Questions

How Do I Get Started in Evangelism?

J. Mack Stiles

CROSSWAY

WHEATON, ILLINOIS

How Do I Get Started in Evangelism?

Published by Crossway
　　　　　　1300 Crescent Street
　　　　　　Wheaton, Illinois 60187

Series design: Jordan Singer

First printing 2024

Printed in the United States of America

Trade paperback ISBN: 978-1-4335-9172-3
ePub ISBN: 978-1-4335-9174-7
PDF ISBN: 978-1-4335-9173-0

Library of Congress Cataloging-in-Publication Data

Names: Stiles, J. Mack, 1956- author.
Title: How do I get started in Evangelism? / Mack Stiles.
Description: Wheaton, Illinois : Crossway, 2024. | Series: Church questions | Includes bibliographical references and index.
Identifiers: LCCN 2023043487 (print) | LCCN 2023043488 (ebook) | ISBN 9781433591723 (trade paperback) | ISBN 97814335917247 (epub) | ISBN 9781433591730 (pdf)
Subjects: LCSH: Evangelistic work.
Classification: LCC BV3770 .S68 2024 (print) | LCC BV3770 (ebook) | DDC 269/.2—dc23/eng/20231228
LC record available at https://lccn.loc.gov/2023043487
LC ebook record available at https://lccn.loc.gov/2023043488

Crossway is a publishing ministry of Good News Publishers.

BP		33	32	31	30	29	28	27	26	25	24
15	14	13	12	11	10	9	8	7	6	5	4	3	2	1

But even if you should suffer for righteousness' sake, you will be blessed. Have no fear of them, nor be troubled, but in your hearts honor Christ the Lord as holy, always being prepared to make a defense to anyone who asks you for a reason for the hope that is in you; yet do it with gentleness and respect.

1 Peter 3:14–15

Are you ready?

> Always being prepared to make a defense
> to anyone who asks you for a reason for the
> hope that is in you . . . (1 Pet. 3:15)

As my wife, Leeann, and I traveled to Bose-man, Montana, we stopped at the Denver airport for a layover.[1] We ducked into the newly opened Smashburger for lunch. While waiting for our meal, I glanced two tables down and spied Lance Armstrong, the disgraced racing cyclist who was stripped of his Tour-de-France titles for using performance-enhancing drugs.

He was eating alone.

"I think that's Lance Armstrong," I said.

Leeann raised an eyebrow, "Honey, could we just eat our lunch?"

"No, no, I want to meet him; I'll be right back."

I walked up to his table and asked, "Are you Lance Armstrong?"

He was mid-bite but nodded and said, "I am." The "I am" came with a question mark—like an implied "don't hurt me."

"Oh, well, Lance," I said, feeling awkward, "I wanted to tell you that I was at the finish line in Paris at the Tour de France in 2004 with my boys, and we saw you cross the finish line in your yellow jersey. We couldn't believe they shut down the Champs-Élysées for the celebration. It was amazing."

Lance looked awkward now too. "I guess your boys are older now," he said.

"Uh, yeah, they're grown men."

"Are they okay?" he asked.

Suddenly, in a flash, I realized how he saw me. He saw me as a fan. I mean, who else would go

to Paris to see the Tour de France with his children? I didn't know how to explain that we were
in France during the race by accident. We had
been traveling back to the United States from our
home in Dubai, and we had some cheapo redeye
tickets that required a fifteen-hour layover in
Paris. Rather than waste time in the Charles de
Gaulle airport, Leeann and I dragged the kids to
the Louvre, bleary and sleepy. Then we exited the
Louvre, lo and behold, onto the Tour de France
finish line. People cheered wildly. I didn't even
know the race was happening. I whipped out
my camera and got a shot of Lance spinning by.

"Oh, the kids are fine, Lance, they're fine,"
I said.

He seemed relieved and sad. Suddenly he
put his head down and said, "Oh, I messed up.
I messed up so bad."

His heartfelt humility touched me deeply.
I felt sad that the poor guy couldn't eat a burger
without having his past dredged up by some
seeming ex-fanboy.

Caught off guard, I didn't know what to say;
I didn't have a plan. I mumbled something about

being a missionary in Iraq, how I followed Jesus, and how Jesus loved giving second chances to people who've messed up.

And then we talked about Iraq a bit, and I said I hoped he enjoyed his burger, and I went and finished mine.

As we took our seats on the plane, I realized that Lance wasn't the only one who messed up. I had messed up. I kicked myself for missing an opportunity to tell a hurting, humble guy, weighted with guilt, the good news of Jesus. Through simple, genuine faith in our resurrected Lord, Lance could be wholly forgiven, restored, and accepted by the maker of the universe.

I trust God's sovereignty. I know the Lord is the one who brings about conversion; it's not my job to save someone. But in that moment, I wasn't ready to do my part of telling others the good news.

I've come to see that most of my evangelistic efforts are failures, like my time with Lance. But the silver lining is that after I blow it, I ponder what to do the next time I have an evangelistic opportunity. Precisely because Jesus loves giving second chances, to me as well as Lance, there's good reason to think there will be a next time.

So let's get ready for evangelism. After all, it's a job for all of us, whether we have recently come to faith or whether we've walked with Jesus for fifty years. In this booklet, I want to give you ten pieces of counsel for how you can get started in evangelism.

1. Start with a Right Understanding of Evangelism

> I did not shrink from declaring to you anything that was profitable, and teaching you in public and from house to house, testifying both to Jews and to Greeks of repentance toward God and of faith in our Lord Jesus Christ. (Acts 20:20–21)

What comes to mind when you hear the word *evangelist*? What about *evangelism*? Before I became a Christian, those words sounded creepy and pushy to me. "Evangelistic zeal" seemed a standard applied to anybody who believed something too much—a wild-eyed and preachy fanatic.

After becoming a believer, not only did Christ become real to me, the spiritual world did too. It dawned on me that much was at stake for a person's soul. So I scrapped negative thoughts of evangelism—but regrettably, I replaced them with an equal amount of religious error.

For instance, I thought evangelistic success meant a person got converted. But that's not true. Faithful evangelism can occur even if nobody positively responds to the gospel. And besides, it's also a discouraging definition since most evangelistic appeals aren't met with positive responses.

Later on, I saw evangelism as an attempt to win arguments for God. But after winning some of these battles, I recognized I was losing the war. Besides offending people with my smug attitude, my apologetic arguments only seemed to move people away from Jesus not toward him.

Next, I attempted evangelism by telling stories about my personal encounter with Jesus— I had a dramatic and scintillating testimony.

Still, people seemed more entertained than convicted of sin.

So after a time—okay, so, after a few years—I looked more carefully at the Bible.[2] Here's a definition I gleaned that has served me for years: *evangelism is teaching the gospel with the aim to persuade.*

I'm sorry it's so simple; I wish it sounded complex and sophisticated for credibility's sake, but that's it—four essential words: teach, gospel, aim, persuade.

Let's look at these four words.

Teach

There are many ways to teach the gospel. It can be taught in a one-on-one Bible study over coffee or a full-fledged sermon on Sunday morning.

There are many things to teach about the gospel. We teach to sweep away obstacles, answer questions, or correct misconceptions. But most of all, we teach to help people see the gospel's truth as the core message of the Christian faith.

Aim

We don't just teach for teaching's sake; we teach with an aim—we desire for something to happen. An aim guards us against seeing evangelism as mere information transfer, a kind of gospel data dump on somebody.

Aim steers us toward the bigger picture. Since much is at stake, we put aside our egos and any hint of dismissiveness—those things that will drive people away—and focus our evangelism on critical components for salvation rather than spinning through needless rabbit trails of theological trivia.

After all, we have the hope that someone might move from darkness to light. So we put ourselves aside for our aim, which is to persuade.

Persuade

The word *persuade* comes from Paul's statement about evangelism in 2 Corinthians 5:11: "Therefore, knowing the fear of the Lord, we *persuade* others."

First, let me state what persuasion is not. It is not manipulation or coercion as some think.

The apostle Paul says, "We have renounced disgraceful, underhanded ways" (2 Cor. 4:2). In the same passage where Paul renounces disgraceful evangelism, he says he refuses to practice cunning or tamper with God's word. In fact, Paul says when we give an open statement of the truth, our words commend us to God and people.

Persuasion helps us see that how we speak is almost as important as what we say. After all, a heated argument rarely persuades anyone. Persuasion means speaking graciously. As Paul says, "Walk in wisdom toward outsiders, making the best use of the time. Let your speech always be gracious, seasoned with salt, so that you may know how you ought to answer each person" (Col. 4:5–6).

Gospel

The final word in my definition is gospel—the very thing we teach and aim to persuade others about. Understanding the gospel requires a bit more thought, so it'll be the focus of our next section.

2. Understand the Gospel Message

> But I do not account my life of any value
> nor as precious to myself, if only I may
> finish my course and the ministry that
> I received from the Lord Jesus, to testify to
> the gospel of the grace of God. (Acts 20:24)

Now that we've got a working definition of evangelism, we need a working definition of the gospel. Here it is: *the gospel is the message of what God achieved in Christ that leads us to salvation.*

When the Bible uses the word *gospel* in the New Testament, it refers to a message about Christ the King who saves his people from their sins. So if we want to get started in evangelism, we need to start with a clear understanding of the gospel.

What Are the Essential Parts of the Gospel Message?

I find it helpful to think of the gospel as a message that answers four questions: (1) Who is God? (2) Who are we before God? (3) Who is

Christ (and what has he done)? (4) And how do we respond to this message?

Of course, massive libraries are filled with answers and explanations to these four questions. But here is the CliffNotes summary:

- *God*: He is a loving Father, he is our Creator, and he is holy, which means that he is wholly perfect and without sin.
- *Us*: We are made in God's image. That is why each person is valuable. At the same time, we are fallen and sinful. The Bible sees those who do not know God as rebels and enemies of God. Though God made us to be with him, our sin separates us from him.
- *Christ*: He is the God-man, fully God and fully man. He lived a perfect life such that he could become the perfect sacrifice for our sins. Jesus, in concert with the Father, agreed that he would become the payment for our sin. His death on the cross satisfied God's justice against our sin and liberated us from the power of sin. He ransomed us from bondage to sin and this ransom is a free gift (Mark 10:45). This means that God

will not hold our sin against us. It means that treasonous rebels can become his children. Jesus rose from the dead, proving his words and life true. He established the kingdom of God on earth and promises to return and make all things new.

- *Response*: We must respond in faith by turning from sin and rebellion and trusting Jesus. Putting our trust in Jesus means believing he is who he said he is and that his way, not ours, is right. Let me put it in the negative: trusting in Jesus means repenting of our disbelief in Jesus. That's how we respond to the good news of what Jesus accomplished for us, and we find salvation.

Even though you could spend a lifetime studying each of these four elements of the gospel, these answers give us a baseline understanding of the good news. All followers of Jesus should be able to communicate in a minute or two these four gospel points.

Every Christian should make it his aim to be a student of the gospel. The apostle Paul's regular method of evangelism was to set out facts of the gospel, answer questions, and overcome obstacles. Paul taught the gospel. To do the same, we need to know the gospel message inside and out.

An excellent place to start is by studying the "big words" found in the Bible concerning the gospel message. How would you explain *redemption*, *justification*, and *propitiation*, among others, in your own words? If you don't know, let me commend reading through a book like Greg Gilbert's *What Is the Gospel?*[3]

What the Gospel Isn't

Since there is so much confusion about the gospel, we also need to understand what the gospel is not.

One of the biggest mistakes Christians make is confusing the gospel with the good things that flow out of the gospel—what we might call "gospel implications." Here's an example of what I mean.

Leeann and I have directed short-term mission projects in many places worldwide. One of the most rugged places was in Guatemala. We took university students to the highlands of Guatemala at the site of the Guatemalan civil war, the so-called Ixil Triangle. We worked in a malnourishment clinic with dying babies. We dug out a fish farm pond so that farmers would have another source of protein besides beans and corn. We inoculated baby chicks. We worked in a medical clinic. The students did all sorts of manual labor. When we returned home and reported on what we had done, we often heard from well-meaning and sweet Christians, "Yeah, that's really the gospel!"

I know what they mean, but when they say that, it puts me in an awkward position. "Well, no," I would respond. "It's not the gospel. It's an implication of the gospel, it flows out of the gospel, it commends the gospel, it adorns the gospel, and it opens doors for us to speak about the gospel, and it's a good thing for Christians to do (though I admit inoculating chickens isn't typically the first thing I think of when I'm trying to commend the gospel!), but it's not the gospel itself." The gospel is a message—news about what the redemption God achieved in Christ's life, death, and resurrection—and we should never let the good works that come from our love for Jesus be confused with the gospel itself.

And since the gospel is a message, it must be spoken.

3. Speak the Gospel

Knowing the fear of the Lord we persuade others. (2 Cor. 5:11)

This passage from Paul's letter to the Corinthians is the basis, in part, for the definition of evangelism I provided earlier. We are about the business of persuading others with the truth of the gospel. And since the gospel is a message, as we have said, we must be able to articulate the gospel in words.

Don't fall into the trap of thinking that living a good life is the gospel. Of course, I want you to live a godly life in Christ Jesus. But doing good deeds without speaking the gospel message only makes people think nice things about you not Jesus, and you alone will never be able to forgive people of their sins.

Saying that you can speak the gospel without words is like saying you can feed people without food.

You must know the gospel, but you must also speak the gospel.

For many of us, this is the most common area of failure in evangelism. Either we don't say anything about the gospel, or we don't speak in a way that helps lead into conversations about the gospel.

For me, evangelism feels like constantly pushing a ball uphill. In almost every opportunity I have to share my faith, I must first make that internal decision to speak up. You will need to do the same. Take that risky step and speak. I find it helpful to remember that awkwardness is better than silence. And the more we talk about the gospel, the more it becomes a natural part of our conversations. The first step in speaking the gospel is deciding to say something about it.

How can you get started? Well, I find it helpful to ask questions like: "Could I explain the core message of the Christian faith to you? I promise it only takes a minute."

I know it can be challenging. So many times I have come to a point when I could have brought up the gospel, and I didn't. So many times I could have brought up something in a conversation that *led* to the gospel, but I didn't.

For example, there is a big difference between saying, "I met someone yesterday that you might know," or "I met someone yesterday *at my church* that you might know."

Decide to be intentional with your words. See where it goes.

Once I was speaking with a young man from Scotland, and he asked me what I did. I said I was a pastor in Iraq. He stared at me wide-eyed and said, "Why would anyone ever want to do that?"

Of course, I could answer in various ways, but I said, "Well, bottom line, I genuinely, deep in my heart, am convinced that Jesus got up from the dead."

His head snapped back, and he looked up as in thought and then said, "Well, fair enough, fair enough."

It was a great place to start a conversation about the gospel message.

"Could I explain the core message of the Christian faith to you? I promise it only takes a minute."

I did, but we talked far longer.

4. Live the Gospel

> I saw that their conduct was not in step with the truth of the gospel. (Gal. 2:14)

According to Paul, we need to live out the gospel. A Christian must align his or her life with the gospel message.

I know I said that living out your Christian convictions is not the gospel.

That's still true.

But did you see that phrase Paul used in Galatians 2:14? He says Peter's conduct was not "*in step* with the truth of the gospel." That's because Paul understood that a Christian responds to the gospel with his or her whole life. It shapes everything about us; it is a path that we walk. Jesus's followers must live gospel-centered lives.

In that same chapter of Scripture, Paul says that his rebuke of Peter, who was out of sync with the gospel, actually preserved the gospel for us: "To them we did not yield in submission even for a moment, so that the truth of the gospel might be preserved for you" (Gal. 2:5). Peter repented by the way; Peter was good at repenting.

There was a time when I thought the gospel was just the doorway for becoming a Christian, and then we moved on to deeper things of the Christian faith, like the second coming (very interesting) or how to have a Christian marriage (very important). But there are two problems with that line of thinking. First, nothing in the Christian life is separate from the gospel; the gospel applies to all of life. And second, nothing is more profound than the gospel.

Rather than just a first step into the Christian life, we should see the gospel as the hub of the Christian life. All the spokes of life lead back to it.

Teasing out Paul's confrontation with Peter also illustrates this point. Peter wouldn't fellowship with Gentiles unless they embraced old covenant ways of life. But the gospel had done away with the old covenant, so essentially Peter was refusing fellowship with Gentile Christians because they wouldn't live in an ethnically Jewish way. Paul was shrewd enough to see Peter's prejudices were, at root, gospel problems, and he spends much of the rest of Galatians sorting that out.

Paul's rebuke teaches us that racial or religious prejudices are a gospel issue. The Bible spells out how we are no longer separated by class, gender, or race, based on a true understanding of the gospel. Because the gospel reconciles us with God, we now seek reconciliation with others as a reflection of the gospel.

Likewise, the gospel has a bearing on your marriage, how to raise your kids, what kind of job you get, and how you treat your neighbors.

A father and friend of mine rebuked his children for some infraction, and after the kids left, his wife said, "Honey, you were right, and the kids were wrong, but I didn't hear the gospel in your correction." She understood that we need gospel grace as we raise our children.

Or think about marriage. Marriage is a mysterious display of the union of Christ with his bride, the church. Paul roots his instructions to husbands and wives in the gospel (Eph. 5:32). Husbands should love their wives as Christ loves the church. Wives should submit to husbands as the church submits to Christ.

You never "move on" from the gospel. It applies to all of life.

So what does this have to do with evangelism?

For me, discovering the gospel-centered life was like being born again, again. Here's how the gospel-centered life connects with evangelism. As we learn how to apply the gospel to every situation, we learn to keep the gospel front and center in our lives. As a result, our love for Christ grows, which means our evangelism grows. My best efforts in evangelism always flow out of my love of Jesus not from a program or a method.

So understand this: Do you want to get started in evangelism? Be so in love with Jesus, so enamored with his sacrifice for sinners, so grateful for the forgiveness of your sins, so amazed with his grace that *you can't help the gospel message coming out of you.* I have found that the more I apply the gospel to my life, the more I tell others about the gospel, and the more I tell others about the gospel, the more I love Jesus. The gospel-centered life becomes a beautiful, healthy spiritual cycle.

If his mercy and love guide your life, you will long to share your faith.

I'm not saying that I get that right all the time. I still have to find my courage to get the words out. That's the next section.

5. Have Confidence in the Gospel

> For I am not ashamed of the gospel, for it is the power of God for salvation to everyone who believes. (Rom. 1:16)

Think about the apostle Paul's ministry for a moment. He faced the dominant Greek and Roman culture's intimidating opposition to his tiny, unimpressive Christian faith. He faced derision from other religions and outright hatred from those of his own religious background.

Yet even in the face of intimidation and threats, Paul kept his confidence in the gospel because he knew the gospel's power. We need to know the gospel to share it. But knowing *the power* of the gospel can motivate our evangelism. It helps us remember that there is inherent power in the gospel message. You may not see it, but we know it to be true because it's proven true in our lives.

Being ashamed of the gospel takes many forms. We fear rejection. We worry about what people will think of us. Sometimes we fear making mistakes or screwing up. Mostly we just keep silent.

Perhaps you've never considered it, but one of the ways we can shrink from evangelism is by hiding behind evangelistic programs and events rather than sharing the gospel ourselves. We think that because we helped set up the hot dog table for our church's neighborhood block party or because we handed out invitations to the Easter egg hunt that we've taken part in evangelism.

Hear me clearly: an evangelistic outreach event is not a terrible thing. By all means, invite people to attend a gospel-preaching church with you. Furthermore, I speak at evangelistic events regularly. For several years, our Christian university fellowship sponsored a Muslim-Christian dialogue on a university campus where we were able to clarify and defend the gospel. But always remember *you* sharing *your* faith with *your* friend is far more potent than any outreach event.

The fact is most people come to Jesus because they heard the gospel in relationship with a friend or family member. In fact, in my experience the people who lead most people to Jesus are not those who speak at evangelistic events but are Christian moms who love their kids!

Besides, no matter how many people come to an outreach event, the event will never be as effective (or as large) as everyone who is a Christian sharing their faith one-on-one with their friends. Think of it this way: a program is to evangelism what sugar is to nutrition.

A little bit is okay, but sugar takes away a desire for more healthy food. When you eat sugar, there's a quick burst of energy, but over time it only makes you flabby and malnourished.

In much the same way, a strict diet of evangelistic programs produces malnourished evangelism.

Just as sugar makes us feel like we've eaten when we haven't, so programs make us feel like we've done evangelism when we haven't.

So let's have less confidence in programs and more confidence in the gospel.

Sometimes it's best to forget the program and just ask someone to read the Bible with you. You don't have to know all the answers. Start with the book of Mark. It's fast-paced, almost like a movie script, and almost everything Jesus does points to the fact that he is the Son of God.

6. Don't Assume the Gospel

> What you have heard from me in the presence of many witnesses entrust to faithful men, who will be able to teach others also. (2 Tim. 2:2)

Paul knows the best way to guard the gospel: entrust it to others who will faithfully pass it on. The fact that Paul teaches Timothy to guard the gospel indicates that he also understands that the gospel can be lost. You can protect the gospel, or you can lose it. Those are the only two options.

The most common way Christians lose the gospel is by *assuming* it. Here's what I mean. Christians assume the gospel when they start seeing it merely as the doorway into the Christian life. Once folks walk through that door, the Christian life is about living a moral life rather than living a gospel-centered one (as I described already).

Once this happens, we fall into the trap of thinking that "nice" people who prayed a prayer or responded to an altar call must be Christians. When a church starts assuming the gospel, anyone who shows up at church interested in "doing ministry" or "being a part of the community" is affirmed as a Christian.

C. S. Lewis noted that at one time the word *gentleman* had a specific meaning. It was a man who owned land and had a title. Over time, it came to mean someone who *acted* like those who owned land and had a title. Eventually, it became a designation on bathroom doors. He went on to explain that the same pattern often happens with the word "Christian." Originally it meant someone who had a personal relationship with Jesus. Over time, it came to mean someone who did Christian things. Nowadays, it designates a political demographic.[4]

A church that assumes the gospel will often preach sermons heavy on moral imperatives but give little attention to the person and work of Christ. It will address the entire audience as believers, even if few in the congregation give evidence of genuine conversion.

Over time an assumed gospel leads to a confused gospel. We confuse external conformity with genuine Christian faith. We confuse basic morality with love for Christ. The cross is treated merely as an example, not the place where God's wrath and love uniquely meet.

It gets worse. The sermon becomes a self-help talk about how to live a better life. All the while, the gospel seems increasingly irrelevant and offensive. Eventually, the gospel is lost—all because the gospel was assumed. Every time

I drive by a mosque or restaurant or museum that used to be a church, I think about how that pattern must have happened in that church.

Here's the pattern:

gospel proclaimed → gospel assumed → gospel twisted → gospel lost

And I'd suggest that the most dangerous part of that pattern is when the gospel is assumed. That's why Paul instructed Timothy to guard the gospel and to pass it on with care. He didn't want the gospel to be lost.

What does this have to do with evangelism? One of the best ways to stop an assumed gospel in its tracks is to make sure we are speaking the gospel to Christians and non-Christians alike.

So you want to be ready for evangelism? Start by pointing your fellow church members to the gospel. It will keep you sharp. Plus you never know who's listening—our children might be attending to our words even if we don't notice.

Make sure that you're listening for the gospel in your church's sermons. I once gave a talk I was particularly pleased with, and I asked Leeann what she thought. Leeann began with a compliment. "That was a great talk." I felt affirmed. Then she said. "But I think you left out the gospel." I was defensive. Later I looked at my notes. She was right. I had started the slippery slope toward an assumed gospel.

The assumed gospel kills evangelism—slay it by having the gospel on your heart and mind and lips.

One of the best ways to guard the gospel is to ensure you have a biblical understanding of conversion. That's our next section.

7. Understand Gospel Conversion

> The time is fulfilled and the kingdom of God is at hand; repent and believe in the gospel. (Mark 1:15)

I lived in the Middle East for twenty years. What a privilege! Sharing my faith with my Muslim friends has been delightful and engaging. It has also sharpened me and challenged me. One of the things that I regularly tell my Muslim friends is that all genuine Christians are converts—simply being born into a Christian family does not make someone a Christian. This idea shocked them!

For Muslims, conversion only entails switching religions. I like pointing them to Jesus's discussion with Nicodemus: "Unless one is born again he cannot see the kingdom of God" (John 3:3). Nicodemus needed to be "born again," and Nicodemus was one of the most religious people on the planet! Being born again, I would explain, doesn't mean converting from one religion to another, though that happens too. Real conversion, truly coming to Christ, means conversion from death to life.

What Conversion Isn't

Sadly, sometimes even Christians are confused about conversion.

Biblical conversion is not:

- Getting your act together
- Tacking a note to Jesus on a tree at a youth camp

- Walking up an aisle or raising a hand following an evangelistic appeal
- Praying a prayer and asking Jesus into your heart

Becoming a better person doesn't make anyone a Christian nor does walking an aisle and praying a prayer with a pastor at the end of a sermon. Anyone can tack a note to a tree or raise their hand at an altar call without genuine faith toward God and repentance from sin. Biblical conversion is not even saying the "sinner's prayer." That prayer means nothing if it's coerced by emotion or peer pressure. Conversion is not a magic incantation.

I once traveled to India with an Indian friend who had grown up there. We attended an evangelistic rally and heard a Western evangelist preach an evangelistic sermon. At the end, he gave an altar call. A hundred people responded. I thought it was amazing—at least until my friend started asking questions of them. It was evident that none of them had a clear understanding of the gospel. "Mack," he told me, "they don't believe the gospel. They just want to be nice to the speaker. They see him as their guest. They're being kind to him, but they haven't repented and believed." I now know people in India who have "converted" a hundred times.

Also, sometimes people respond to a "gospel" that has very little to do with the gospel described in the New Testament. Some preachers and evangelists offer a gospel that promises a carefree, prosperous, happy life; or sometimes ministries employ famous people to convince enamored crowds that Jesus is the way to success; sometimes people leave out parts of the gospel they think are unpalatable (such as repenting). But conversion doesn't happen with a dose of bribery, hero worship, or a half gospel. It occurs only when the Holy Spirit moves in a person's heart and creates faith and repentance upon hearing the simple, true gospel message.

The gospel is good news of how we can receive forgiveness of sins through the death and resurrection of Christ. The only saving response to that message is the first words of Jesus recorded in the book of Mark: "Repent and believe" (1:15). That's how we tell people to respond to the gospel. That's what biblical conversion entails.

I know God can use things like altar calls and the "sinner's prayer" to help people come to a place of repentance and belief, and it's terrific if that's what God used in your life. God hits straight with crooked sticks. Still, if we want to be faithful evangelists, we need to avoid the temptation to make people do something that looks like conversion but isn't.

If we don't have a biblical understanding of conversion, then we'll end up affirming false conversions, we'll wrongly give assurance to people who think they are Christians who are not, and we might assume some people are believers who are actually lost.

What Conversion Is

Conversion is supernatural. God reaches into our lives, rips out our stone-dead hearts, and gives us new hearts alive to God. Consider how Paul describes conversion in Ephesians 2:

But God, being rich in mercy, because of the great love with which he loved us, even when we were dead in our trespasses, made us alive together with Christ—by grace you have been saved. (Eph. 2:4–5)

Conversion involves being brought from spiritual death to spiritual life. It means that we will determine to follow the way of Jesus in faith for the rest of our lives. True conversion is always followed by the fruit of repentance that lasts a lifetime.

Paul says in Romans 10:9–10,

If you confess with your mouth that Jesus is Lord and believe in your heart that God raised him from the dead, you will be saved. For with the heart one believes and is justified, and with the mouth one confesses and is saved.

I understand the difficulty of calling people to repent. To be told that you are dead spiritually, that you're wrong about the life you're living, and that Jesus is the only way to God are some of the most offensive claims of the gospel to modern ears.

But don't shrink back; press in.

8. Be Bold and Clear with the Gospel

[Pray] also for me, that words may be given to me in opening my mouth boldly to proclaim the mystery of the gospel. (Eph. 6:18–19)

When Paul was in jail, his prayer request was for boldness in sharing the gospel.

If I had found myself in a Roman jail awaiting possible execution, I think my prayer request would be for God to get me out!

But not Paul.

Paul doesn't share many prayer requests in the New Testament, but half of them, by my count, were concerned about sharing the gospel with boldness and clarity. If Paul, one of the most fearless evangelists ever, needed prayer for his evangelistic efforts, how much more do we?

I've lived and traveled through some dangerous places: riots in Kenya, bombings in Iraqi Kurdistan, and devastating illnesses in

Guatemala. Neighbors threw rocks through our windows in Tunisia because we were Christians. Naturally, I would ask others to pray for our safety—there's nothing wrong with that. But the longer we lived in the Middle East, the more I felt the need for boldness rather than safety. Looking deeply into my heart, I saw how easily I shrunk from speaking the gospel boldly and with clarity. Eventually, I began asking people to pray for us, not about safety, but about being bold and clear with the gospel.

Boldness and clarity can be giant roadblocks to effective evangelism. There are many reasons we're not bold and clear. Perhaps we've not taken the time to burn in our memory the short gospel message. Sometimes we're so intimidated we bumble around, much like I did with Lance Armstrong. Sometimes we fear rejection, or we're afraid we'll say the wrong things. There are a host of reasons we might be unclear or timid.

But the overarching reason we shrink back from proclaiming the gospel is that our fears intimidate us. Here's the solution: trust God and take more risks. Jesus loves risk because we're stepping out in faith in his word. So slay the fear of man! Not only does it open doors to speak of Jesus, but you'll also find that taking risks in evangelism is a key to your spiritual health. Be ready to talk with those God brings your way— they are divine appointments.

At a church lunch in Boston, I participated in a Q&A session on evangelism. I enjoy the give-and-take of those kinds of events.

A soccer mom raised her hand. "I'm so busy," she said, "I don't know how to fit evangelism into my schedule."

Typically, I would answer questions such as hers with another question. The dialogue that ensues is always the same.

"When you are at your kid's soccer game, do you sit alone?"

"No."

"Do you have conversations with the parents of other soccer players?"

"Yes."

"Then think about trying to share your faith with them there!"

On this particular occasion, however, I decided to dispense with the inductive approach. The main issue is not time or opportunities but a heart posture of fear. I simply responded: "Take more risks." I repeated it slowly. "Take—more—risks."

Then I said, "Next question?"

The main reason we don't share the gospel isn't because we lack time or opportunities. We have a heart issue. We fear man. So pray for boldness, trust God, and take more risks.

For the next hour in that Q&A, we spoke on many topics concerning evangelism, but those three words are what people remembered. Nothing else I said seemed to stick, but that phrase did. And that is because the lack of evangelistic risk is why most of us miss evangelistic opportunities.

9. Pursue Gospel Love and Gospel Unity

There are so many tools for evangelism. There are outreach events, multi-million dollar ads on TV, and books that explain the Christian faith. (I've written some of them!) But there is one tool for evangelism that surpasses them all—a loving community. Your local church is your most essential tool for evangelism. It might not seem true, but look at what Jesus says:

> By this all people will know that you are my disciples, if you have love for one another. (John 13:35)

Just a few chapters later, Jesus prays that his people will be marked by unity "*so that the world may believe that you have sent me*" (John 17:21).

What a thought! Jesus says the love we have for each other in the church is a statement that we are truly converted and disciples of Jesus, and when we are unified, we show the world that Jesus is the Son of God.

When God formed the church as his embassy on earth, he built into its very fabric an evangelistic witness to himself: the church's love and unity.

So many have tried to make church relevant to the culture around them. I understand their desire and at one level even want to affirm it. You don't want to plant a Farsi-speaking church in a place without an Iranian population, for example.

But we must not miss the bigger picture. We cannot redesign the church for the sake of evangelism. Jesus knew what he was doing when he designed the church. We should follow Christ's command and strive to love each other in our community and work hard for unity as a body of believers.

And as we do so, let's trust that Jesus did not forget the gospel when he built the church. Cherish the things that God wove into the church to proclaim the gospel: things like baptism—the picture of Jesus's death, burial, and resurrection—which also signifies that his death is our death and his life is our life. Cherish the Lord's Supper, which proclaims the death of Christ until he returns. Each Lord's Day as the church gathers, we hold out the gospel: we pray the gospel, sing songs that proclaim the gospel, and most of all, we preach the gospel.

Many Scripture passages instruct and shape our evangelistic efforts. But these two verses from John are foundational. They show us that loving other Christians affirms our genuine conversion to Christ and that uniting with other believers shows that Jesus is the Son of God.

A young mother from Iran, named Zahra, met a woman in our Iraqi church named Lindy. They formed a friendship, and Lindy faithfully shared the gospel with Zahra. After some time, Zahra came to faith in Christ.

The church was overjoyed with Zahra's commitment, especially knowing the sacrifice it was for her to leave her Muslim faith to follow Jesus.

Zahra desired baptism, and we were overjoyed to bring her into our local congregation. We filled up our plastic kiddie pool in the front of the building we used for a church, and I baptized Zahra.

Not only did the church witness her baptism, but so did her husband, Ali, and their nine-year-old son. Ali was not a believer, far from it. Zahra's baptism was the first time he had attended church. But he was open to his wife's new faith, and it was clear he cherished her.

Later that week, Ali wrote me. I expected him to tell me what he had learned from my sermon. (I thought I had preached a powerful sermon!) But he didn't mention a thing about it.

Instead, in broken English, he told me that our church service was a potent event in his life. The main thing he noticed was that we loved each other. He said that he had never seen people loving each other across boundaries—our little congregation had members from twenty different nationalities. Some of our members came from countries that were at war with the countries of other members. Yet, to Ali's shock, they loved each other. He couldn't get over the unity of our church. Everyone seemed to be in agreement with each other about Jesus.

There it was: love and unity.

Eventually, some of Zahra's radical cousins found out about her conversion and began issuing death threats to her, Ali, and even their son. They were hounded out of Iraq and fled to France. But her cousins chased them to their hiding place and forced them to flee again—this time to a refugee camp.

I lost hope that Ali would come to faith in Christ; with his suffering, it seemed impossible.

After all, Ali had lost his home, job, and car, and lived in a distant refugee camp far from his home all because his wife believed in Jesus.

But it was there, through the faithful witness of his wife and the love and unity of another local church, that Ali came to faith.

Don't miss your part in the evangelistic nature of the church. You are called to love your fellowship of believers. You are called to be unified. You do this not because they are lovable or sinless or because they treat you well. That's how pagans love. You do this because Jesus tells you to; more important things are at stake than our natural human tendencies to love only a specific group. Loving, genuinely loving, those who are not like you in your local church shows that you are truly Jesus's disciple, holding him out as the Savior, Lord, and hope of the world.

10. Just Do It

I hate to sound like a sneaker commercial but just do it.

The best way to get started in evangelism is to take a step with someone you know: a relative, friend, colleague, or classmate.

Will you feel uncomfortable at times? Sure, we all do. But remember, awkward is better than silent. And as you share your faith, you will get better at it.

Here's a quick plan:

(1) Write on a Post-it note the names of at least two people you know who do not follow Jesus and pray for the opportunity to share the good news with them. Pray earnestly for them. God loves to answer the prayer, "Lord, use me to share your good news." Stick the Post-it note somewhere you will see it. And keep praying.

Then, (2) take the risky step to text, call, or email, or better yet, ask face-to-face if you could get together. Say something honest, like I would love to talk with you about spiritual things. Don't start with a hard case; go for low-hanging fruit. For example, look for someone who has come to your church and seems to be inquiring about Christianity.

(3) If you meet up with a friend, tell him or her you would not be a good friend if you didn't share the joy (love, purpose, meaning, etc.) you have found in Christ.

Ask questions about what he or she thinks about God or Jesus.

Then consider leading out with the question I mentioned before: "Has anyone ever told you the core message of the Christian faith? I can do it in a minute."

(4) Have a follow-up plan. It may just be to get together again. The best follow-up is to ask if your friend would read the Bible with you. I like reading the Gospel of Mark with people, but any Gospel is good to read with a seeker. You don't have to know all the answers; just read it, and if someone asks you a tricky question, don't make something up; say, "I don't know, but let me find out." Ask the Lord to lodge the truth of Scripture in your friend's heart.

(5) Consider reading a book with your friend as well. I've already mentioned *What Is the Gospel?* by Greg Gilbert. Or consider reading my book *The Truth about Lies: Why Jesus Is More*

Relevant Than You Think.[5] It's a simple, winsome book that helps correct common misconceptions about Jesus and Christianity and explains genuine faith.

Finally, don't be discouraged. I've found that 99 percent of my evangelistic attempts don't end with someone becoming a Christian, but remember the story Jesus told—he searches out the one lost sheep out of a hundred, and he will use you to do the same.

Recommended Resources

Greg Gilbert, *What Is the Gospel?* (Wheaton, IL: Crossway, 2010).

Mack Stiles, *Evangelism: How the Whole Church Speaks of Jesus* (Wheation, IL: Crossway, 2014).

Mack Stiles, *Marks of a Messenger: Knowing, Living and Speaking the Gospel* (Downers Grove, IL: InterVarsity, 2010).

Mack Stiles, *Speaking of Jesus: How to Tell Your Friends the Best News They Will Ever Hear* (Downers Grove, IL: InterVarsity, 1995).

Mack Stiles, *The Truth about Lies: Why Jesus Is More Relevant Than You Think* (Leyland, UK: 10Publishing, 2023).

Notes

1. When possible, personal stories in this booklet are shared with permission from those involved, and some names have been changed for privacy.
2. I also had some help from J. I. Packer's excellent, short book *Evangelism and the Sovereignty of God* (Westmont, IL: InterVarsity, 2012).
3. Greg Gilbert, *What Is the Gospel?* (Wheaton, IL: Crossway, 2010).
4. See C. S. Lewis, *Mere Christianity* (New York: Collier, 1960), ix–x.
5. Mack Stiles, *The Truth about Lies: Why Jesus Is More Relevant Than You Think* (Leyland, UK: 10Publishing, 2023).

Scripture Index

 **9Marks**

Building Healthy Churches

9Marks exists to equip church leaders with a biblical vision and practical resources for displaying God's glory to the nations through healthy churches.

To that end, we want to see churches characterized by these nine marks of health:

1. Expositional Preaching
2. Gospel Doctrine
3. A Biblical Understanding of Conversion and Evangelism
4. Biblical Church Membership
5. Biblical Church Discipline
6. A Biblical Concern for Discipleship and Growth
7. Biblical Church Leadership
8. A Biblical Understanding of the Practice of Prayer
9. A Biblical Understanding and Practice of Missions

Find all our Crossway titles and other resources at 9Marks.org.

John
Onwuchekwa

Church Questions

Sam
Emadi

Church Questions

Mark
Dever

Church Questions

IX 9Marks

How Can
I Grow in
Hospitality?

...eel Like
o Church?

...sen

Keri
Folmar

Church Questions

IX 9Marks

How Do I Get
Started in
Evangelism?

Mack
Stiles

Church Questions

IX 9Marks

How Can
Women T...
the Local

Keri
Folmar

Church Questions

IX 9Marks

Who's in
Charge of
the Church?

...ized?

Sam
Emadi

Church Questions

IX 9Marks

How Can
I Serve My
Church?

Matthew
Emadi

Church Questions

IX 9Marks

How Can
I Love Ch...
Members
Different...

Jonathan
& Andy N...

Church Questions

IX 9Marks Church Questions

Providing ordinary Christians with sound and
accessible biblical teaching by answering
common questions about church life.

For more information, visit crossway.org.